ARCHITECTURE OBSERVED

by Alan Dunn

ARCHITECTURAL RECORD BOOKS • NEW YORK

Published by Architectural Record, a McGraw-Hill Inc. publication.

330 West 42nd Street, New York, New York 10036

This book designed by Arthur Hawkins

Supervisor of production: Stephen M. Miller

Library of Congress Catalogue Card Number: 75-165515

SECOND PRINTING, MARCH 1972

SBN: 07-018305-8

Alan Dunn—caricature by Mrs. Dunn

FOREWORD

Alan Dunn's work and mine have appeared side by side in The New Yorker and in the Architectural Record; and I have long wanted to tell Dunn how much I have enjoyed and admired his work. But where shall I begin? Shall I say that he is obviously a better architect than the architects whose fashionable clichés and grim follies he exposes? Or shall I say that his urbane satiric style, deft but merciless, puts him in a class by himself; for this is what has been missing from contemporary criticism in all the arts. All this is true; but it is not enough. It is the style of his mind that I would praise, and the wittiness of his draughtmanship. Happily, the viewer of these pages needs no further help from me to find out how Dunn has cleared the air for us by his laughter.

Lewis Mumford

YOU CAN'T GO HOME AGAIN

At the turn of the century a child was born in a dreamy, gingerbread-gothic house in Belmar, New Jersey, not from choice but because his mother was on her summer vacation. In his winters he lived in a New York City brownstone, the interior of which was a pandemonium of Victorian, Biedermeier, Art Nouveau and wickerwork.

The boy was nurtured on the warmth and charm of Ruskin's Seven Lamps of Architecture, Sesame and Lilies and The Stones of Venice so he was ill-prepared for the architectural apocalypse that was to come.

Form suddenly followed function rather than tradition; a new sun had arisen on his horizon. Enchanted by the new-found freedom he strode forth only to collide with a concept of space whose hidden boundaries still whispered, "Conform!"

Nursing his multiple contusions he marveled as form followed fad and a dazzling panorama of creative anarchy spread over the countryside. But what had become of stability?

Is architecture a result of one's times or is it a directive toward better living? The great minds have not as yet congealed on this point so why not just curl up in a bean-bag chair, bemused and confused, and enjoy man's predicament in coping with an environment that is always changing and always will? If you love it it will love you back. I love it.

Alan Dunn

CONTENTS

"What's the use of living in the country if you never go inside and work on the garden?"

"One thing more—it still takes a heap o' livin', you know."

"Run for it, Phyllis, Myrt, Paul, Gwendolyn, Towser—Power failure!"

"There! Now do you still roll?"

"And this is our—ah—picture window."

"It's from Junior and now he says he's going to 'attack the total environment'—
I think that's a crack at us—"

"Hey, what's going on up there!"

"Of all the nerve! They're going to build an oil-storage tankyard next door!"

"Close and secure all primary wall openings, slide the sunlight roof to full closure, fasten down the canvas weather screening and close all secondary ports—it's beginning to rain."

"Twas the night before Christmas and all through the contained space . . ."

"Children!"

"I can't find my house!"

"She's gone—said she wouldn't live under the same hyperbolic paraboloid with me."

"Dinner is served, Madam."

"Well, all I asked for was a roof over my head."

"If you can't stand the heat, get out of the Open Plan!"

"Children!"

"You know how it is—money keeps getting tighter."

"What I love about these new shopping centers is their landscaping!"

"Instead of giving us a stained glass memorial window, how about an air-conditioning package?"

"You'll be glad to know we've finally achieved one-man installation—Now there's just a little matter of stand-by pay for the local building unions."

"You and your 'sense of insecurity'!"

"What's cooking?"

"We built it of reflecting glass—not knowing—"

"Have the photographers gone?"

"But I can't just leave it here—You have to sign for it."

"Boy did they pick our brains!"

"You solved the Urban Center transportation problem perfectly but, by the way, whatever became of the Urban Center?"

"There isn't a damn thing we can do. They claim it's Pop Architecture!"

"No—this *is our factory—That's just our new pollution-control unit.*"

"Watch where you toss your cigarette butt, Mac!"

"To be fair, I have to admit Boston Baked Beans aren't what they used to be either."

"I'm certainly getting tired of this 'Because it's there' idea!"

"Do you think I like *being buried in the heart of town*, two miles from the nearest shopping center, three miles from the drive-in movies, five miles from the airport . . ."

"What do you have to do to become a Model City?"

"Oh, Mr. Mies! Tenant on the 34th floor brought his own window shades!"

"*Never mind. On thinking it over we decided to let it age.*"

"What do I knock on for more radiant heat?"

"Whoever thought of reducing taxes on buildings that spent ½ of 1% on fine art certainly didn't think it through!"

"Landmarks Commission, I think!"

"This is the last word in condominiums—Each owner hires his own architect."

"What'll I do with it—put it down the incinerator?"

"It happened during the night—pure vandalism, I think!"

"Now this was built in the days when people were afraid to walk the streets at night."

"Save the Capitol!—Save the Robie House!—What about me?"

"Leave it to the Joneses—75-degree angles!"

"*Don't worry—If you love it enough it will love you back.*"

"Architecture dates you—We live in a Happening."

"It's designed on the principle of the Möbius strip, which has neither an inside nor an outside. We're praying for a mild winter."

"I don't know how to break it to Paul, but my mother saw it and she loves 'every little nook and cranny'."

"Can you show us which is outdoors and which is in? Just in case of fire, you know."

"It's very 'todayness' is what I like—but what about tomorrow?"

"Merely a matter of jacking it up—We certainly weren't going to be outdone by the Joneses!"

"*Are you sure you saw it move?*"

"I think they're just trying to stand out!"

"Do I have to live in a 'statement?' Can't I just have a home?"

"And then I found that the latest cliché was 'to avoid all clichés'."

"You knocked?"

"He broke the box alright—if that's any consolation."

"That one is for small talk."

"Remember when we eliminated the 'cornice'?"

"You and your module! The Joneses are now living in a capsule!"

"Just at I feared—our client has a Louis Seize mind in a Louis Sullivan body."

"They want a de-controlled environment, panic locks, better fenestration, indoor-outdoor syntheses . . ."

"So the more rational the structure, the more irrational the mural—Do I make myself clear?"

"I just stopped by to tell you how much I loved your thing at the Fair!"

"Please just a small potted climber or two—we don't want to lose our membership in The Ivy League."

"Just what do you mean by 'stressed skin'?"

"How does he ever expect to be an architect if he can't invent a new roof?"

"A ha, privacy! So you want to spend government money on frills."

"Since you appear to be a thoroughly intelligent, happy and integrated couple, I am afraid I'll have to turn you down—My houses are supposed to solve a problem."

"Sheer genius! What Pollock did for painting, he's doing for architecture."

"Try thinking of it as 'space cadence' and maybe you'll feel better."

"Do I have to go through Kandinsky to get to Modigliani?"

"Yamasaki may have started something, but you certainly finished it!"

"I'm afraid the architect didn't analyze our needs—he analyzed the needs of the state!"

"Hey, slow it down!"

"Of course I fed it the right data—Call IBM and hurry!"

"Whose going to tell them 3,750 homes have to be recalled for defects?"

"Affleck, Desbarats, Dimakopoulos, Lebensold, Sise? We have a cornerstone problem here . . ."

"What, eleven lightning rods?"

"Only six months ago this was a 'Blighted Area'."

"Well, I warned them slip-forming wasn't here to stay."

"Next time you go home at night, don't forget to close the roof!"

"The way they build partitions nowdays, I'll never get my work done!"

"Close that door!"

"That's technology for you—prestressed adobe!"

"And while I was in the States, I met this fellow named Buckey Fuller."

"OK—We sent them the Temple of Dendur—Now what's to prevent them from sending us Grand Central Station?"

"This is one movie that's not going to be made in Italy."

"With what Pericles spent on this he could have eradicated all the slums of Athens—but you know human nature."

"Technical Aid, I think—Government architect from Washington. He suggests we move the facade out 40 ft."

"Well, for heaven's sake—brutalism!"

"And here we have one of the earliest known forms of lift-slab construction."

"You and your 'better worlds'!"

"'Man'!"

"A nice try, but notice how it never got off the ground?"

"Open it again! They're still inside!"

"You should have thought of starlings before you ordered the new mural!"

"As if I didn't know!"

"I feel a little silly calling it 'the old Alma Mater'."

"I must say, the radio-relay people were certainly co-operative about 'regionalism'."

"When are they going to remove the scaffolding?"

"The Ford Foundation—right?"